All That I Am To Be
"A WOMAN'S WORTH"

INSPIRED WHOLENESS LLC
KANSAS CITY, MO 64138

All That I Am To Be
"A Woman's Worth"

All rights reserved. No portion of this book may be used without written permission of the publisher, with exception of brief excerpts for magazines articles, reviews, etc.

Copyright © 2008 Paulette D. Hubbert

Inspired Wholeness LLC
www.paulettehubbert.com

ISBN 978-0-9793091-5-1

LCCN 2007921436

DEDICATION

This book is dedicated to my parents. To my mother Edna M. Hubbert who taught me my worth by living her life as an example of a woman of worth, and to my father, Willie L. Hubbert for always demanding that I honor my worth.

A special dedication to my sons Anthony and Marcus, my favorite men. The two of you are my heartbeat.

ACKNOWLEDGMENTS

I would like to thank my Aunt Paulene (my second mother), for her hours of dedication and assisting me with various aspects of this book, and her never-ending words of wisdom and encouragement throughout my life.

Jackie, what can I say, thank you for your friendship, your devotion to this project and for always having my back.

Veronica, I can always depend on you to tell me what I need to hear vice what I might want to hear. I know "you got me". After all, that's what friends are for. Thank you for your tireless efforts on this project.

Anetra, thanks for always cheering me on.

Christy, thank you for your assistance on this project, your enthusiasm, and never-ending encouragement for me to write this book.

I believe that God allows people into your path, some for a season and some for a lifetime. There are too many to list that have made deposits in my life. Deposits that have helped to shape and mold me into the person I'm called to be, a woman of worth.

ABOUT THE AUTHOR

Paulette is a native of Kansas City, Missouri. She is the 3rd born of 7 children, and the older of two daughters. Paulette is a retired Marine and a single parent of two boys, Anthony and Marcus.

Paulette is a Professional Life Coach, Licensed Clinical Social Worker, (LCSW), Certified Substance Abuse Counselor, and a Certified Prevention Specialist. She holds a Masters in Social Work (MSW), and an undergraduate degree in Social Psychology.

She has over 20 years of experience in the areas of; Leadership Development, Management, Program Development, Education, Prevention Education, Social Work, Mental Health, and Substance Abuse.

She also has over 20 years experience in developing and conducting numerous seminars, trainings and workshops on various subjects. (Examples: Leadership Development, stress and anger management, women issues, self esteem, substance abuse, family dynamics, substance abuse and the family). Her experience encompasses over 20 years of working with diverse groups and populations in various settings: Corporate, Military, Educational environments and Clinical settings.

Her passion is motivating and assisting others in living a balanced life and being everything they have been purposed to be.

CONTENTS

Preface	11
The Rose	13
This Journey	15
My Journey	17
Chapter 1 Your Perception, Your Reality?	23
Chapter 2 Doing What You Fear	35
Chapter 3 How Much Do I Love Thee…	51
Chapter 4 Going Deeper	63
Chapter 5 Spiritual Nourishment	73
Chapter 6 I'm So Into You	86
Chapter 7 Serenity	95
Chapter 8 Moving Out of Your Comfort Zone	105
Chapter 9 Bringing It All Together	115
Individual and group exercises	123

PREFACE

This book has come about by what I like to term as "divine inspiration". I believe that all behavior is purposeful. I have worked in various clinical settings and with diverse populations of woman from around the world, and from all walks of life. These women were women with issues that stemmed from them not knowing their value. The common thread that I have found amongst these women was that because they didn't know their value, they compromised their worth. Because they compromised and settled for less, their mind, body and soul were compromised, which opened the door for a host of issues and problems. You will continue to get what you have always gotten, if you continue to do what you have always done. My prayer is that by reading this book, women everywhere and from all backgrounds, ethnicities and walks of life, will begin to do something different.

I am writing a second edition of this book just a year after the release of the first book due to the overwhelming response to the first book. Women from all over have responded in ways that I would have never imagined. They have spoken words like healing, restoration, understanding and love that they have found for themselves by reading the words contained inside the pages and, have asked for more.

Our words are powerful, and they affect our thoughts, beliefs and behavior in ways that can only be described or brought forth by our actions. To be all that you are to be you must find balance in all that you are.

This second edition is only the beginning of a new and exciting journey that each of us must take individually at some point in our life. It is a compass to assist you in finding direction and focusing on your path.

The Rose

The rose universally symbolizes love and beauty.
In order for a rose to grow it must to be placed in an environment that will cultivate its growth. It requires pruning to rid its self of parts that no longer serve its purpose. It requires light as a source of energy to bring forth its beauty to show the world.

In order for you to come forth as a symbol of love and beauty, you must plant yourself in environments that will continue to cultivate your growth. You must reflect on the parts that block your light, and prune those parts that no longer serve you. It is then, through your source of energy, your light, that you will reflect your purpose and bring forth your beauty to show the world.

This Journey

I've journeyed many places, seen a lot of faces, but none like this place before. I've journeyed here, there and every where, but none like this place before. I've journeyed many roads, with twist and turns, near and far, but none like this place before.

I've journeyed to foreign lands, traveled the world, from city to city, state to state, and land to land, but none like this place before. I've journeyed to places of happiness and pain, of hope and despair, but none like this place before.

This is a journey of places unknown, where secrets are kept, stones are unturned and territories unexplored. This is a place that I will never leave, a place where hope and dreams are made clear ……born from a place deep within, where the spirit dwells, and peace is filled. A place of strength, love and joy abound. I've journeyed to a place that I can call home, but none like this place before.

My Journey

Many painful experiences have brought me to the point that I am today. Through all of my trials, tribulations, obstacles and victories I have come to realize that God has been my source of strength, my comforter, counselor, teacher, provider, protector, father, and friend. It is God that I give credit for who I am today, yesterday, and who I will be in the future.

I was raised as a Christian, but now I realize that at the beginning of my journey I really didn't understand what being a Christian really meant. I had only been practicing Christianity the way I had seen others practice the faith. I didn't know God for myself and didn't understand that I was supposed to "know him". However, I did know enough to pray.

I had been praying for God to heal me, to restore my life, and to help me understand why my life was falling apart. I had asked him to show me why I continued to find myself in familiar circumstances. At that time my life it was chaotic at best. I was at a point where I didn't care what it would take to feel whole, to be complete, I just wanted change.

It was 1999 and I was driving along the Beltway in the Washington, DC area. All of a sudden it hit me. The memories came rushing in like a tidal wave and there was no way to stop them. I suddenly remembered the pain. All of the negative consequences that come with living life on life's terms and all the feelings that come with those experiences.

Feelings of abandonment, isolation, loneliness, frustration, disappointments, shame, guilt, anger, rejection and a host of other negative feelings that all add up to fear. I realized that I had been surviving instead of living. I had been living in fear. Fear of living my life the way that God had intended for me to live. Fear of walking in abundance and letting my light shine.

My life was falling apart and I finally understood why. I understood how I had been looking for love in all the wrong places. I understood why I kept doing the same things, expecting different results, but always ending up in the same place. I finally understood why I didn't feel loved, even though I was surrounded by it. I realized that I had been depressed for most of my life but didn't know it. I finally understood it all and I cried.

I pulled over on the side of the highway and I cried. I cried until my blouse was drenched with tears. I cried until I had used a package of tissues blowing my nose. I cried until my head hurt and I couldn't stand it anymore, and then I cried some more. I cried for all the times I had been hurt, disappointed, criticized, rejected, felt lonely, shameful, guilty, unloved, or left alone. I cried until I couldn't cry anymore, until the tears dried up on my face, and my eyes were red and swollen and nothing else would come.

Then I cried some more, but this time it was cleansing tears. I cried for what was to come. I cried for the healing and restoration that I knew was taking place, and I cried for the revelation and the journey that I was about to begin. I cried for how my life was going to be. Filled with joy, freedom, and abundance, but most important, peace. I cried tears that I had never cried before because it was that day my spirit was reborn, the day I was set free.

Then I cried out for God to continue to heal me to make me whole. It was that day that I vowed to God and to myself that I wouldn't turn around. No matter what the cost, if he would keep me, I would go forth. I would do whatever it was going to take for me to remain free, to be whole, to heal from all the past pains, and sorrows. I vowed that I would not accept any more chaos in my life. I promised that I would walk in all that he has for me and I vowed that I would trust him. I vowed that I would be the woman that he has called for me to be. Then I put my car back in gear and drove home. But I knew that I had been changed.

I use to lead a song in the children's choir called "I've been changed". One of the verses said I've been changed and rearranged. Our choir director use to tell me to sing that song with attitude, that I had to sing it with conviction so that others would know that there was no doubt in my mind that I had been changed. That day, in that moment, I had attitude. I couldn't explain it, but I knew beyond a shadow of doubt that I had been changed and rearranged, and that no matter what, there was no turning back.

I began to embrace the pain because I knew that out of the pain my healing would come. Not just healing but wholeness. I knew that I would walk with my head held high, with no apologies, and no excuses for who I am or who I was called to be.

I wish I could say that it was all over and I lived happily ever after that day, but that's not the case. Understanding something and putting it into action are two separate roads and if the two are ever going to meet it's going to take some work. Instead of instantly living my life happily ever after it became even more chaotic.

Once you've been set free, truly set free, you're willing to pay the price, any price, to remain free. I had been set free that day and I wasn't willing to give up my freedom. I was free from the inside out and I wasn't willing to trade that for the sake of anything or anyone. I had it all and I walked away from everything I had ever wanted, everything that added up to the American dream. I realize now that up until that point security was what had been most important to me, my driving force, and I had been paying the cost for that security. The expense was my peace of mind, my worth. I wasn't willing to settle anymore.

Most important, I couldn't continue to be an example to my children that it was "OK" to settle for less than what you can be for the sake of being. I wanted to be an example to them that you could have it all and not have to settle or compromise any area of your life to have what you deserve.

Because we are children of God it is our birthright to live in abundance. Up until that day I had not been a good example for my children of how to live life in abundance. I wasn't quite sure how I was going to teach them the opposite, but I did know that if God was for me, who could be against me. So, I set out to discover who I was and how to live life more abundantly. However, my life couldn't start over until I confronted my pain and all the issues I had created in my life in the pursuit of happiness.

Until that day on the Beltway I was sure I had resolved all of my issues. Instead, I had just buried most of them deep within. Because I had buried my issues instead of resolving them, I was ripe for picking anytime the right situation or circumstance was present to trigger those issues. Once triggered, my unresolved issues would come out in my attitude and behavior.

God has a funny way of showing you yourself when you don't want to deal with the issues in your life. The issues that prevent you from walking in your purpose. He used others to show me who I was. At the time of my revelation I was a substance abuse counselor. As a counselor you help others deal with all of their heartaches, pain, disappointments and fears.

Many of my clients would come to me seeking counsel on the very issues that I hadn't resolved. At the time, I wasn't aware and hadn't acknowledged their issues as my issues. (The irony is that I helped many resolve their issues.) My clients had been the catalyst for change in my life. At the time I didn't know or realize what had taken place. God had used my client's as an instrument of change, to stir up all of those issues I thought I had "taken care of".

I am a child of God and I believe in the Trinity. My belief in my Lord and Savior Jesus Christ is the essence of my being of which my beliefs, values, and morals are based on. He is my yesterday, my present, and my tomorrow. I am dedicated to becoming everything that God has called me to be. Although life has dealt me many painful experiences, I now thank God for those experiences. It was through the pain that I have come to know Him, and can honestly say that He heals all wounds. My faith in God has not always been as strong and ever so present as it is now. It is through my journey that I have been able to find strength in him.

    I am not sharing my faith in God or my life lessons to try and persuade you to adopt my beliefs, faith, Christianity or even a specific denomination. I am simply sharing what has been my source, or rather who has been my source of strength throughout this journey of healing and restoration that I am about to take you on. However, I do invite you to embrace God as you know and understand him as we begin this journey.

Chapter 1

Your Perception ... Your Reality

(Or Is It?)

Memories

Did I just say what I thought I said, or do what I thought I did? All these thoughts running through my head, I'm not sure what I did. Did it happen yesterday, or some time long ago? I'm not sure what's going on, all these thoughts that won't let go. They are all going on in my head, it seems all at one time, but I'm sure it won't be long before they all calm down.

Did I hear what I thought I heard, or see what I thought I saw? My mind is so confused with all these thoughts, I don't know if it's even me, or where it all went wrong. Unaware of all the thoughts that happened yesteryear, unable to recall, I'm not sure where they've gone. Somewhere buried deep within, but I'm sure they won't stay buried long. One wrong word, a simple look, or someone says goodbye, all the memories come flooding back just like they were never gone.

I want to start by asking who do you spend most of your time with? Who is the one person you can't get away from? If you spend the most time with you, shouldn't you like yourself, love yourself? Like being with you?

We often don't walk in our purpose because one, we don't know our purpose, and two, because of our own self-defeating thoughts, behaviors and attitudes about ourselves. When we don't know, how can you walk in your purpose and live out your true potential.

How do you determine your worth, your essence? Worth is defined as value. In philosophy, essence is the attribute (or set of attributes) that make an object or substance what it fundamentally is. It can refer to physical aspect or attribute, or to the ongoing being of a person (the character or internally determined goals).

When you know your worth and are walking in your true essence, you can be truly happy as a result of how you feel about yourself and perceive the world. That is when you find true happiness, contentment, and peace with others and yourself. Simply put, it is everything about you. It's about honoring yourself so that the quality or qualities that make you who you are, mind, body and soul, come shining through. When your mind, body and soul are balanced, you show your true essence.

In order to be truly happy, you must be content with yourself. We often go through life looking for love in all the wrong places. Where we need to start is within. If we are not a hundred percent, we can't give a hundred percent, nor can we expect a hundred percent in return.

So, who are you? What's your purpose? How do you bring that purpose forth in every area of your life? Some of you already know the answer, some of you have an idea but haven't quite reached the mark, and some of you....you are still searching. My hope is that you will either find confirmation that you are on the right path, gain more clarity or that you will be able to begin your journey of who you are and discover your true worth.

To determine your worth, you first have to look at the mind and how it works. Our minds work on a conscious and subconscious level. Our conscious mind can only hold 5-9 thoughts at one time in the conscious. It then does a data dump to our subconscious.

Our subconscious stores every experience that we have ever had from the moment of conception. It constantly records our experience, environment, things that are done and said to us and around us. Anything you have ever been exposed to, heard, or seen has been recorded deep within. Those recordings happen through feelings, sight, hearing, smell and taste. Because our subconscious holds all of our life experiences it also influences our thoughts, actions and behaviors whether we are aware of it or not.

Have you ever met someone that you felt you had met before but you couldn't remember where? Have you ever had an experience that frightens you, but you were not sure why? Have you ever wanted to change a behavior or habit and despite your best efforts, you somehow continue the behavior or habit you want to change? When information is recorded into the subconscious it remembers the circumstances, however, isn't able to make distinctions between various situations.

Most of my life, until recently, I was afraid of heights. To stand over a large open body of water would almost send me into a panic attack. Not heights in general, only when I was high above the ground and there were no railings or something similar that added extra security. I mentioned until recently because during a workshop that I attended for helping trauma victims, I had a flash of a baby in a pamper hanging over a tub.

Upon further investigation, my mother told me of a story that when I was two, she had run some water in the bathtub. When the phone rang she went to answer it and suddenly heard my older brother screaming. She ran back into the bathroom to find him hanging on to my pamper. I was hanging over the tub with my face in the water. My brother kept me from completely falling in, but he was too small to pull me out. Hence, I discovered my fear of heights when there were no barriers or safety precautions to keep me from falling in.

My subconscious mind only remembers the fear, the danger, and the trauma associated with that event. It wasn't able to distinguish or gage the level of danger, or even if there was danger. Although I had no conscious memory of the incident, whenever the right circumstances were in place, my subconscious would remember the danger, and trigger the fear of being in an open space, in danger, without safety rails in place.

Our thoughts, morals, values, beliefs, coping skills, behavior and daily function first come from our subconscious thoughts. Our first lessons in life on how to act, talk, what to say and do, are learned from those with who we are in direct contact. Our families are our first direct contact. They are our first social system that we are introduced into in which each family member interacts with each other in a predictable, organized fashion. The family's function is to meet social, educational, and health care needs of each family member. The family social environment involves situations, circumstances, and working toward a common goal that includes the basic needs of all human beings.

Socialization is the process of teaching children the values, roles, and behaviors of their culture. This process continues throughout life although the fundamental building blocks begin during childhood. The Social learning theory states that people learn or acquire their behaviors through their social environment, with the family environment as the primary agent of socialization. We are all products of our environment. Unless we are exposed to something different or taught something different, we function from the framework of that environment (good, bad or indifferent). As children, we learn by seeing and acting accordingly.

Family dysfunction is any process in the family that limits the effective development of family members. An environment where there is mental abuse, physical abuse, sexual abuse, mental health issues, substance abuse, or domestic violence will be contributing factors that intensify negative beliefs, thoughts and values. Stressful events can have negative psychological effects that can follow us into our adult life.

Research has shown that dysfunction in the family of origin may affect several areas of an individual's life, three areas are: problem solving, communication and distress in intimate relationships. Research suggests that the degree of family dysfunction in the family of origin is not just the presence of family dysfunction, it is related to interpersonal distress.

Many people believe that emotions are primarily determined by our experiences. If your environment is out of balance, you function out of balance. Your emotions and thoughts will be out of balance. Your life lessons are your very core from which you function. Your core beliefs are sometimes rooted in self-doubt, low self-esteem, guilt, anger, shame and a host of other self-defeating beliefs about yourself that prevent you from moving forth and living a balanced life.

All behavior is purposeful. Because those beliefs are rooted in the subconscious, what is in you will come out, even in times when you would like to act a different way or respond to a situation in a different way. Until you learn to do something different, to obtain a different result, you continue a vicious cycle of self-defeating behavior and self-fulfilled prophecy about your abilities, talents, and potential.

As a child your environment, family, friends, teachers and society in general teaches you how to react to any given situation. The response to those thoughts, feelings, and beliefs are stored into your subconscious. Let me give you an example.

When a child is sexually abused many changes take place, not just physically, but emotionally and more specifically subconsciously, whether it is one encounter or reoccurrences. That child, at that moment, makes several decisions about that experience. They can fear, not trust, decide that sex is bad, is not supposed to feel good, or they may decide that they don't like sex. They can also experience fear in a complete opposite way. They may take from that experience that you should trust everyone, or believe that sex is the way to obtain love and approval.

The circumstances in which the abuse occurred, the individual, and how that message is perceived will dictate the beliefs about the experience. The beliefs and all of the feelings associated with the experience are then stored in the subconscious or subconscious memories. Once rooted in the subconscious, that individual will act according to what that experience meant to them, often times unaware of the subconscious decisions and beliefs that have taken place. Because the shift is subconscious they are unaware of how those decisions and beliefs affect their behavior.

Where does the shift in beliefs come from? It can be as complicated as abuse, or as simple as being told (or convinced) to believe something negative about you. Once rooted in your beliefs you will begin to operate from a place of fear, and from there, the negative behaviors and beliefs will surface.

I once worked with a client who was Valedictorian of her high school class. She also graduated from college magnum cum lade in her undergraduate and graduate class, and was making a six figure salary in the corporate world. However, she suffered from low self-esteem and depression. The root cause was that she thought she was stupid despite the evidence. After all, all of her life her parents had told her that she was stupid. Growing up, they constantly reminded her that she would never amount to anything, and that she had the sense of a fly. Why wouldn't she believe them? They were her parents!

Another client had decided that she wasn't a good mother despite the fact that she had a very loving relationship with all three of her children. Her children described her as loving and caring. They also stated that they never wanted for anything. And all three children were consistently on the honor roll. Despite the evidence, she decided she wasn't a good mother because she was a single mom, she had to work, and her children needed a father of which she couldn't provide.

Society had taught her that children needed two parents in the home in order for the children to thrive. Her decision that she was inadequate affected her ability to be decisive, which led to procrastination, which led
to anxiety and stress. Is your perception reality or a distorted reality based on circumstances you are unaware of?

IF YOU WERE TO KNOW, WHAT HABITS OR SHORTCOMINGS DO YOU HAVE THAT YOU WOULD LIKE TO CHANGE?

WHERE DID YOU LEARN THOSE HABITS OR SHORTCOMINGS?

WHAT EVIDENCE DO YOU HAVE THAT THOSE SHORTCOMINGS ARE REALITY?

WHAT IS YOUR REALITY?

USE THIS SPACE TO WRITE ANY THOUGHTS OR AWARENESS THAT YOU HAVE HAD ABOUT YOURSELF. BEGIN THE SENTENCE WITH: I REALIZE OR NOW I UNDERSTAND...

CONTINUE TO WRITE ANY THOUGHTS OR AWARENESS THAT YOU HAVE HAD ABOUT YOURSELF

Chapter 2

Doing What You Fear

Into The Light

When I do what I do, how can I fear, when you promised me your presence is near? When I'm filled with the light, how can failure appear? You said go forth and I'll be there. No room for unhappiness, or despair, because beyond me light is there. Illumination, brilliancy, unscathed and untouched, there is no room for fear when light is about.

Come into the light for the time is near, no room for circumstances, situations, chaos or fear. Into the light where joy is present. Into the light where peace is near. Into the light where healing takes place. Into the light where darkness can't stay. Into the light where you will find rest.

Our greatest fear is usually our greatest asset. Webster defines fear as an unpleasant often-strong emotion caused by anticipation or awareness of danger. When we embrace that fear we act accordingly.

Fear is the basis from which all other negative feelings flow … low self-esteem, self-doubt, self-fulfilling prophecies etc. Fear immobilizes us and prevents us from moving forth in our purpose. Once our thoughts, emotions, and beliefs are rooted in fear we begin to use words like always, never, should, can't, must, etc. In our day-to-day vocabulary we subconsciously incorporate those words into a context that works against our goals, dreams, aspirations, and our purpose.

Let's look at those words from a negative connotation. **Always:** forever, at any rate, in any event, never, not ever, at no time, not in any degree, not under any condition. **Should:** ought to, must, will have to. **Must:** requirement, be unreasonably or perversely compelled to. **Can't:** to be unable to do otherwise. These words and others are definitive words that mean it has been decided. What you have thought or spoken in any given situation is the final decision. There is no room for flexibility or a different outcome because the final solution has been determined before you even begin. Hence, you will act accordingly and your outcome will be as you speak. How often have you said I can't, I might fail, I'm afraid? God does not give us the spirit of fear, but that's the mode that we usually operate from.

Fear can convince you that you're not good enough, smart enough, pretty enough, talented enough…, When you're walking in fear you self-sabotage in many different ways through your words, attitude and behavior. Words and phrases like can't, never, always, should (it should be this way or that way) or we are always a victim of circumstances, nothing ever goes right for me.

Procrastination is a big one. If you never get started you can't fail, right? Wrong! Sometimes the failing is in never trying, because then your left with wondering what would have happened if I had just tried. Once you start the would've, could've, should'ves those beliefs then take root and bring on thoughts and feelings of guilt, shame, fear, focusing on the past and a host of other negatives beliefs become a vicious cycle. You then continue the pattern of self-defeating thoughts and behaviors. It's like a car, when one part malfunctions or stops working the way it was designed to work, and you don't address it, it affects the entire functioning of the car.

An example: I once worked with a client that would make comments that she would never be happy. Although her desire was to be happy, joyous, free. Out of fear (feeling inadequate, low self-esteem etc.), she subconsciously decided that she would never be happy, joyous, free; told herself she would never be happy joyous free and spoke that she would never be happy, joyous, free, and, consequently had bouts of depression. She existed in an overall depressed state about her life and circumstances. Even when things were going well because she unconsciously decided that she would never be happy based on a set of circumstances that had happened early in her life.

We make decisions based on our negative core beliefs if we are not aware. All are rooted in fear and continue to spill over in every aspect of our lives, subject to recall at any time. The subconscious compartmentalizes those areas that are too painful to think about until something happens ... an emotional trigger occurs to bring it forth.

A trigger can be words, ideas, statements, sounds, sights, taste or smells that can set off a strong emotional reaction. They can be conscious or unconscious triggers that go to the depths of pain, frustration, confusion, guilt or shame. Everyone has triggers. The key is being aware of them, what they are about or what caused them, and learning how to manage them instead of them controlling you.

Emotional triggers are created by your environments, or by a specific event, or, series of events that have happened in your life. They can occur naturally, and, sometimes on a daily basis. For example, a trigger can be something as simple as hearing a certain tone or sound, or a familiar voice that brings back specific memories of a time in your life. It can be a positive or negative memory. Any time you hear that sound you are instantly taken back to a certain memory or set of memories. When this happens, you react to the memory and sometimes relive the memory as you think of the events and experience the feelings associated with that memory.

An emotional trigger is automatically executed in response to certain events. Triggers can be subtle and most often are. That is what keeps you unaware and responding to certain situations in a certain way. Once the trigger is stored in your subconscious, or you make the decision that a situation or circumstance has to be a certain way, you act accordingly.

These are your emotional triggers or obstacles that cause you to stagnate in fulfilling your purpose. When you are faced with similar circumstances that caused you to accept the negative belief about yourself, your subconscious automatically triggers the negative belief and brings forth the negative thought or feeling to your conscious without you being aware. You then respond or begin to operate based on the thoughts and beliefs that the trigger brings forth. When you operate from those triggers you engage in self defeating behaviors.

What are your triggers that are buried in your subconscious, that immobilize you and cause you to make negative decisions or react in a negative way, that set you on a path of self-defeating behaviors that you would like to change? Where did they come from? What evidence do you have that supports that belief, or allows you to continue to operate in that belief?

The chart on the next page begins to look at beliefs and behavior that are rooted in your subconscious when a negative event occurs, or, a trigger happens, or, if someone has convinced you to believe something negative about yourself. These beliefs have become stored in your subconscious. You may identify with some of these beliefs or have your own. Starting with fear, and working out, identify those beliefs which leads to your self-defeating behaviors?

BEHAVIORS

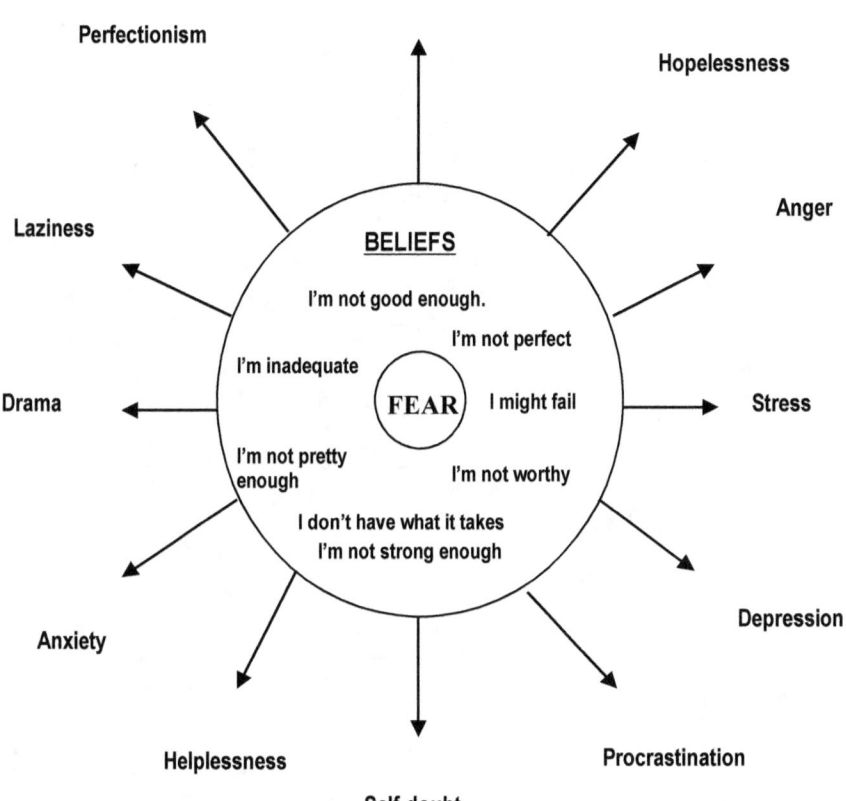

WHAT'S IN YOUR CIRCLE OF FEAR?

BEHAVIORS

USE THIS SPACE TO WRITE ANY THOUGHTS OR AWARENESS THAT YOU HAVE HAD ABOUT YOURSELF. BEGIN THE SENTENCE WITH:
I REALIZE OR NOW I UNDERSTAND…

As you begin to identify those triggers, think about where you first learned that belief. Was it reality or a distorted perception of reality? When was the first time you felt inadequate, not strong enough, not smart enough, not pretty enough? Another way to ask that question is who told you or where did you learn that you were inadequate, not strong enough, not smart enough, not pretty enough, etc? What messages did you receive about who you are and what you would accomplish in life? Take some time and answer each of these questions to each trigger that you have identified. After you answer the question, ask yourself was this reality or perception? What emotions are tied to those triggers?

Let's go back to the client that decided that she was stupid. All of her life her parents constantly reminded her that she was stupid and that she would never amount to anything. Because she was convinced that she was stupid, despite the evidence, she believed that she was. Once she made the decision that she was stupid, she subconsciously set out to prove that she wasn't and had done an awesome job in establishing the proof. However, she wasn't able to consciously be aware of the proof because her thoughts and beliefs had been rooted in fear. Imagine the change when she examined the evidence and decided that she wasn't stupid.

When our thoughts and beliefs are rooted in fear, it can also have the opposite affect. I have worked with clients that believed they were products of their environment. They believed that fate had made the decision for them to live a certain life, or be a certain way. For example: I had a client whose mother was an alcoholic and had lived her entire life in abusive relationships. Her grandmother was also an alcoholic and lived in an abusive relationship. For as far back as she could remember alcoholism ran rampant in her family.

All of the women who had been role models in her life drank, used drugs, and/or experienced some type of abuse. She described the women in her family as lazy, inadequate, and that they had never been able to accomplish anything. Hence, she had been convinced by her environment and circumstances that she was destined to be an alcoholic, become lazy, inadequate, never accomplish anything, and that abuse was a way to express love. She had never considered anything outside "the norm", or the possibility that there was another way of living.

Imagine the shock of learning that she could do something different. Once she identified her fear of failure, inadequacy, and learned that love wasn't supposed to hurt, she was able to see that she did have the potential to be successful. She stopped drinking, left her abusive relationship and began to live a life that she previously had only dreamed about.

Another question to ask yourself: how have you allowed someone else to define who you are or who you have to be? How much say did you have in that decision or did you just accept what had been decided for you?

When we are not aware of our true worth and identity, as well as our divine rights, we live in fear. Light is the opposite of fear. What positive beliefs do you have about yourself? When you focus on the positive beliefs you can become whole and produce positive results. As you can see your beliefs, values, thoughts and behaviors affect who you are.

Now that you are beginning your journey of understanding how you sometimes make decisions rooted in fear, you can choose to focus on your positive attributes, rooted in light and make decisions rooted in positive beliefs. Surround yourself with liked minded people that will support and encourage you to do your best, people that will help bring out your best.

The chart on the next page can assist you in identifying your strengths and those unique qualities that you may or may not be aware of that you possess. It illustrates who you can become when you let your light shine. It is an example of your worth and your true essence. Again, start from the center where your light shines and work out to beliefs and then behaviors.

If you have difficulty identifying your strengths ask for assistance from people around you that support you in a positive way. Think about compliments you have received about yourself and write those down. Ask family and friends that know you and that you trust what positive qualities they see in you and write those down.

BEHAVIORS

- Love
- Confidence
- Respect
- Safe
- Happiness
- Peace
- High Self Esteem
- Assertive
- Security
- Joy
- Abundance
- Motivated

BELIEFS

- I am loved
- I'm good enough
- I am enough
- I am liked
- I can....
- I'm smart
- I am pretty
- I like myself
- I can succeed
- I love myself

LIGHT

COMPLETE YOUR OWN CIRCLE OF LIGHT

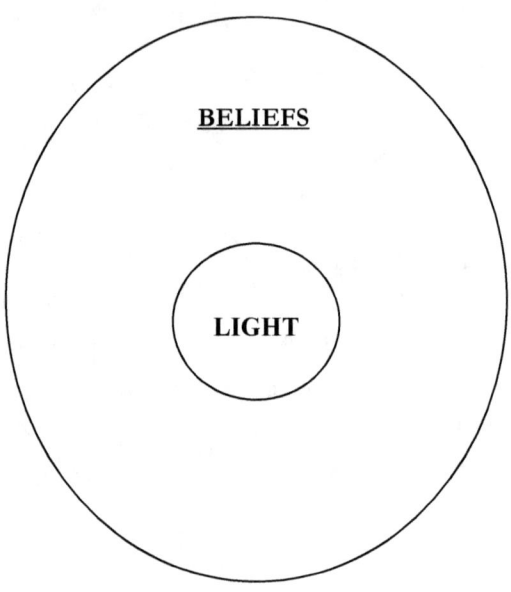

WHAT IS YOUR GREATEST FEAR?

HOW HAS THAT FEAR PREVENTED YOU FROM MOVING FORTH IN YOUR PURPOSE?

HOW CAN YOU BEGING TO PRODUCE POSITIVE RESULTS IN YOUR LIFE? BEGIN EACH SENTICE WITH THE POSITIVE RESULTS IN MY LIFE ARE......

USE THIS SPACE TO WRITE ANY THOUGHTS OR AWARENESS THAT YOU HAVE HAD ABOUT YOURSELF. BEGIN THE SENTENCE WITH:
I REALIZE OR NOW I UNDERSTAND...

Chapter 3

How much do I love Thee...

I Am Who I Am

You don't know who I am, my journeys, my fears, my heartache, my pain.

You don't know me, you haven't bothered to find out, who I am, or what I'm all about. One glance at me and you assume... you size me up, you take no time to find out who I am, or what I'm really all about.

Doubts and fears they come and they go, but no matter what, I know what I know, who I am and what I'm all about. For such a time is this I'm called to be, the me that I am determined to be. But you don't know me, you don't understand, no one else can be the me that I was called to be, the me that I am.

I am a woman of worth, of value, a treasure beyond compare. If only you would take time to see the internal qualities that God has placed inside me, they are beyond measure, beyond compare. If only you could see who I am, you would know that you are in the presence of a gem.

Don't take me for granted or you'll soon find out, that I make no apologies for what I'm about. Don't get it confused, my confidence exudes, my presence I embrace with no apologies, or excuses, for I do what I do, and I am who am.

Throughout history women's sexuality has molded and shaped our consciousness, roles and often our worth. A woman's physical attributes have often tipped the scales to the amount of influence and/or power, or to determine worth, instead of inner qualities, talents or attributes being the determining factor. Mind and spirit are often neglected. Although times are changing in some arenas, we still have a long way to go before our worth won't be determined by how well we wear our jeans. Society tells us what they want us to think, what to know and how to act. Because we believe that as women it is our job to serve, we often times do what is expected of us, instead of questioning or challenging what we are told.

Because of how we are defined, we often pay a high price for self-esteem and self-worth. When our mind, body, and spirit are compromised, or out of balance, our worth, value and qualities are compromised. At times the damage can be not only detrimental to our well being, but our behavior destructive to those that we come in contact with.

When we make decisions out of fear, and settle for less than our worth to "fit in", be accepted, or loved, we allow those fears to define who we are, instead of whom we are called to be. By compromising our worth we justify the feelings and fear of inadequacy, I'm not pretty enough, good enough, strong enough, smart enough, etc.

We attract who we are. When mind, body and spirit are out of balance it creates internal and external conflicts. When we compromise and go against what we have been called to be, internal conflict begins.

We often choose men, friends, and acquaintances that justify how we feel about ourselves. We choose those that can validate and often justify our internal and external conflict.

The internal conflict can cause depression, anxiety, self-doubt, hate, guilt, shame, disrespect of ourselves and others, aggression, feelings of unworthiness, feeling unloved and going to extremes to feel loved, and host of other mental turmoil. Once the internal conflict begins, we have to define our behavior with external explanations. The external explanations can be a willingness to compromise our value and morals. We accept abuse (emotional, physical and sexual), promiscuity, withdrawal, isolation, compromise of oneself, settling, disrespect, drug abuse and a host of other thoughts and behaviors that affect the very core of our being. The internal and external conflicts create a vicious cycle that exacerbates our condition and behavior. We begin to create baggage and carry it around subconsciously, out of fear. It can be dangerous to look for love in the wrong places without a sense of worth and the ability to validate your own worth.

It is impossible to validate worth or to recognize worth when you don't know your worth, when you're operating from a place of fear. It's like trying to sell a car but being unsure of its value. Let me ask you this, if you had a brand new home, your dream home, everything that you ever wanted in a home, would you sell it for a dollar? What about $100? You wouldn't sell it for less than its value. Would you even be looking to sell? You wouldn't sell unless you didn't know it's worth or you were desperate (for whatever reason) and was willing to settle for less.

If we place that much value on material items, and are willing to do the work to know its value (whatever it may be), why don't we place that kind of value on ourselves? We are willing to spend hours shopping for the perfect shoes, the perfect outfit, but don't spend any time on determining our worth or the "perfect us". When you operate out of fear it becomes difficult to make decisions that are right or perfect for you. It is even more difficult to become that perfect you.

The "perfect you" are that person you were created to be. What makes you perfect is you were created to fulfill a purpose that only you can fulfill. No one else can do it for you and you cannot fulfill someone else's purpose. That's the perfection.

Look at it from the perspective that we are all a piece of a larger puzzle. If you have ever put a jigsaw puzzle together, you know that every piece has its place and no other piece will fit in another place. That piece is perfect in its own right because it has a place that it fits into, placed perfectly, and no other piece will fit. That's what makes it perfect.

Why are we willing to settle for less than our worth? We settle for less because we don't know our worth. Another reason is that we have made decisions from a distorted perception of ourselves. When the decision of our worth is from a distorted perception, our worth is decreased and we believe that we don't deserve better.

I once supervised a young lady who had "a reputation". One day I came to work and found her in the bathroom in tears because she had just found out that she had "a reputation". As we began to talk, I soon discovered that she didn't have a clue as to who she was, nor was she able to determine her worth.

Out of her brokenness, as a result of her environment, and the subconscious decisions she had made about herself, her worth was defined by having a man in her life. It didn't matter what man, any man would do. The way to win his love was by "making love to him". The proof that she had won his heart was for him to simply say that he loved her. It didn't matter if they had dated for months or if they had just met, the key to her heart and her legs were to say that he loved her. There didn't have to be any other proof, all she simply needed to hear were the words "I love you".

Again, can you imagine the shock when she discovered she could make the decision to love herself and be content with herself. By learning to love herself, her self-esteem grew. Once her self-esteem grew she was able to not only make better decisions about men, but better decisions about her life.

The external changes can only happen when the internal begins to make changes. You will find your perfection in your purpose, you're worth. Begin by asking yourself what is my worth and how do I find my perfect place or purpose? Begin determining your worth by making a list of what you're grateful for, focusing on your talents, your attributes, and your light.

Make a list and post it where you can see it everyday. Make your qualities and attributes one of the first things you think about when you wake. Post it somewhere so that the list will be one of the first things you see when you wake, as a reminder of your worth. Begin to remind yourself throughout the day of your talents, attributes, your light

WHAT INTERNAL CHANGES NEED TO TAKE PLACE?

CONTINUE TO WRITE INTERNAL CHANGES THAT WILL TAKE PLACE?

**USE THIS SPACE TO WRITE ANY THOUGHTS OR AWARENESS THAT YOU HAVE HAD ABOUT YOURSELF. BEGIN THE SENTENCE WITH:
I RELIZE OR NOW I UNDERSTAND...**

USE THIS SPACE TO WRITE WHAT YOU'RE GRATEFUL FOR. BEGIN THE SENTENCE WITH: I AM GRATEFUL FOR...

CONTINUE TO WRITE WHAT YOU ARE GRATEFUL FOR

USE THIS SPACE TO WRITE YOUR ATTRIBUTES AND TALENTS. BEGIN THE SENTENCE WITH: I AM...

CONTINUE TO WRITE YOUR ATTRIBUTES AND TALENTS

Chapter 4

Going Deeper

Broken

How deep will this go? No one seems to know. Deep within I continue to change unaware that shifts have taken place that affect my mind, my body and my soul. How will I know how deep it goes? How will I know when I have changed, when the pain continues to grow? The faint memories are constant change, unaware of how they go.

Now that I know my brokenness …brokenness that flows and resides within. I won't compromise, broken and disgusted, I have to let go, of all the thoughts that cause me to feel low. I'll be the me that I choose to be, no more decisions will be made for me. My choice is of purpose and deliberate delight. No more subconscious thoughts, no more sleepless nights.

I cry out to you my God, let the comforter come and speak peace be still, let your healing power flow and fill the depths within. And when your mighty power flows, memories that are deep within, memories of the distant past will be remembered no more. I don't care what it takes, now that I know my past, now that I know my brokenness…brokenness you have got to go, you can't dwell here any more.

We naturally play different roles or parts at different times, in different situations (mother, daughter, friend, wife, boss, etc). We begin life in wholeness. When events happen that can cause pain or fear, it creates brokenness and the different roles that you play are carried out from a place of brokenness. When information is recorded into the subconscious your beliefs generate your behavior that causes you to play different roles from a place of wholeness or brokenness. Those roles are rooted in fear or light and your values and morals.

Your values are your feelings, and your moral structure is the way you order your values. When your values are aligned you operate from a place of light and harmony. However, if brokenness occurs your values can become distorted and your mind, body and spirit become unbalanced.

If your value is love, your decisions are usually based on love and the ability to achieve that love. If your beliefs about yourself and others are distorted and rooted in fear, your decisions and behaviors based on love will be distorted and rooted in fear.

When you have an emotional significant event happen, subconsciously brokenness occurs as a means of protection, survival, defense, etc. When negative beliefs are formed, unhealthy boundaries are formed in our subconscious. Once the unhealthy boundaries are formed, circumstances will happen to test and reinforce those negative beliefs and strengthen the unhealthy boundaries. Subconsciously we make decisions based on our brokenness and establish unhealthy boundaries instead of from a place of wholeness. On the next page is an illustration of wholeness. The second circle is an illustration of brokenness.

Illustration:

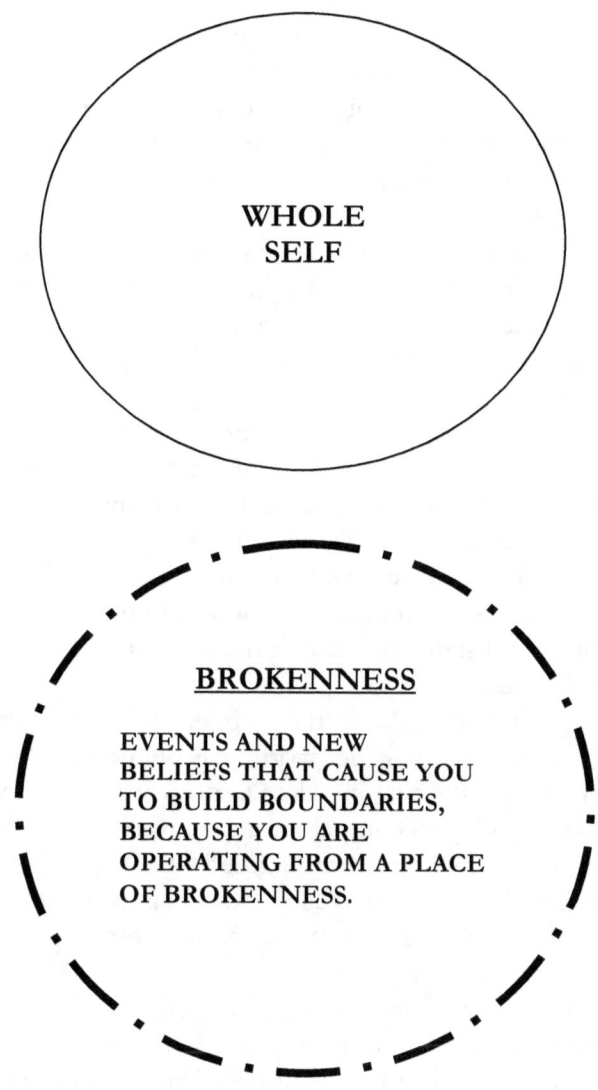

In this case, brokenness is not the issue, it's the behavior. When unhealthy boundaries are formed we operate from a place of brokenness, hence, our behavior can become negative and destructive.

Let's go back to someone that has been sexually abused and grew up in an environment where the only way love was expressed was through abusive behavior. In that moment, during those experiences, several decisions were made and unhealthy boundaries were formed based on those experiences.

If one of her highest values is love, she will operate from that value out of fear and a distorted understanding of love. She could have learned any combinations of lessons from that experience, but let's say the lesson she learned was that in order to be loved, sex had to take place.

She then sets out on a journey to find love and having sex becomes the means for finding that love. She becomes promiscuous. She offers herself up to anyone that she feels will show her love in the way that she understands love and how one should receive love. Many women have been misunderstood and become the victim of degrading name-calling and status because of misunderstanding their brokenness.

What she learned in that experience was to compromise her worth or worse, her worth was defined by that experience. Because she didn't know her worth and didn't have anything to compare healthy love vice unhealthy love, her unhealthy boundaries defined what she understood as love, and how to receive love, which in turn dictated her behavior. In other words, her values were displaced and her worth compromised.

Here's another example: I worked with a client who was in a very abusive relationship. Prior to the meeting her boyfriend she lived alone, traveled and was just enjoying life. However, she had been taught that she had to have a man in her life in order to be complete. She also believed that she couldn't achieve financial security unless she had a man in her life. She had been convinced, and the decision had been made for her, that any man in her life was better than no man. Her worth was defined by having a man in her life. Although she valued freedom and actually wanted freedom, security was a higher, more dominant value.

At the moment she accepted that decision, unhealthy boundaries were formed, and she compromised her worth and settled despite the evidence. Because she didn't believe she could make it on her own she wouldn't leave the relationship. Her distorted perception prevented her from seeing the evidence that she already had the security she was seeking.

How do your beliefs align with your values? You first must determine what they are. On the next page or on a separate piece of paper, rate the different areas of your life. Spirituality, Relationships, Significant Other, Profession or Work, Finances, Personal Development and Your Health.

Then arrange each area in order of importance from one to eight. Ask yourself what is important to you about each area of your life? Then write the first five words that come to mind about each area. Prioritize each of the five sets of words in each area from one to five. This will give you a general picture of your values.

Then answer or even write down how each area of your life, according to your priorities and values, are in alignment with your beliefs and behavior that you completed in chapter two. What changes do you need or want to make? What areas are you happy with? How can you continue to build and strengthen those areas?

LIFE RATING SCALE

On a scale of 1-10 rate each area in accordance with your level of satisfaction with where you are today. 1 being I would like to make changes, 10 being I'm satisfied.

Spiritually - I have a sense of well being or peace (I am spiritually connected).

1   2   3   4   5   6   7   8   9   10

Professionally - You have achieved, or are achieving your goals, and you are utilizing your gifts and talents.

1   2   3   4   5   6   7   8   9   10

Personal growth - Your personal growth, development, and self discovery (you continue to evolve and love who you are).

1   2   3   4   5   6   7   8   9   10

Rest and Relaxation - You take time for yourself to relax, rejuvenate, and enjoy leisure time.

1   2   3   4   5   6   7   8   9   10

Finances - You're financially secure. Your content in respect to giving and receiving, abundance.

1   2   3   4   5   6   7   8   9   10

Physical wellness - In overall good health, sense of physical safety

1   2   3   4   5   6   7   8   9   10

Primary relationship - I am content with being/not being in a primary relationship.

1   2   3   4   5   6   7   8   9   10

Primary relationship - I am content with my primary relationship.

1   2   3   4   5   6   7   8   9   10

Relationships - I am currently content with other relationships (friends, family, and associates).

1   2   3   4   5   6   7   8   9   10

USE THIS SPACE TO RATE EACH AREA OF YOUR LIFE

USE THIS SPACE TO PRIORITIZE EACH AREA YOUR LIFE

WHAT ARE YOUR STRENGTHS (NAME AT LEAST THREE, DO NOT INCLUDE ANY PHYSICAL ATTRITRIBUTES)?

USE THIS SPACE TO WRITE ANY THOUGHTS OR AWARENESS THAT YOU HAVE HAD ABOUT YOURSELF. BEGIN THE SENTENCE WITH:
I REALIZE, OR, NOW I UNDERSTAND…

Chapter 5

Spiritual Nourishment

Surrender

Lord, Lord, help me run this race until the race is won. You said that you would carry me when I couldn't carry on. The stress and strain, the struggle and strife at times seem too much to bear, but Lord if you will walk with me, I will have the strength to carry on, I'll have the strength to care.

My body is getting tired, my mind is getting weak, and my soul needs some rest. Lord will you carry me so I can do my best? I give it all to you right now, those things I can not change, because your love covers all, I can't possibly fall. No looking back, no turning around, speak to my spirit, to me oh Lord, so that I can heed your call.

Where do you get your spiritual nourishment? Although religion and spirituality are interconnected, it is important to make the distinction between spirituality and religion. Religion is a personal set or institutionalized system of attitudes, beliefs, practices or rules that an individual adheres to. It is the rules, beliefs and rituals that (generally) involve a faith in a spiritual nature, and a study of inherited ancestral traditions, knowledge, and wisdom related to understanding human life.

The term "religion" refers to both the personal practices related to faith as well as larger shared systems of beliefs. In other words, it is the vehicle that one believes gives them access to their God and allows for the expression of that belief.

Spirituality concerns itself with matters of the spirit. It is a sense of connection to something greater than oneself, which includes an emotional experience of religious awe and reverence. Equally important, spirituality relates to matters of sanity and of psychological health. It focuses on personal experience. Spirituality is an innate need. It is the qualities or characteristics that are a part of your inner nature. It's who you are and how you govern yourself. When your behavior and beliefs contradict with your spirit, your values are compromised. I believe that we all were born with the potential for greatness, a greatness that is waiting to be born out of our purpose.

Because religion and spirituality are interconnected, it is important to examine our religious practices and beliefs to determine if they are congruent with the way that we express ourselves in our daily lives. Are you walking in the truth? Are you aligned with your beliefs, rules and expression, or is there a spiritual disconnect?

Here is an example: In Christianity we have the Beatitudes. They are a code of ethics for all Christians. The Beatitudes are the internal essence of your spirit. The Beatitudes tells Christians how to be blessed and teaches that position, authority and money are not important, what matters is faithful obedience from the heart. That's not to say that you can't have position, authority and money, but it has to come from a place that is in alignment with faithful, obedience from the heart.

The Ten Commandments are the rules that Christians are suppose to live by and assist in regulating the Beatitudes. The Ten Commandments provide guidance and give structure in to the way that Christians are supposed to live. We were created to be in tune with spirit. Ideally, spirit should be expressed in the way that we live. Our mind, body, and spirit must work together in harmony if it is going to be expressed in the way that we live. If mind, body, and spirit are not in alignment, then there will be a disconnect, or distancing of spirit and you become unbalanced.

When the beliefs (The Beatitudes), are not following the rules (the Ten Commandments), mind, body and spirit are out of balance. If unbalanced, subconsciously there could be feelings of guilt, shame, unworthiness or a host of other self-defeating thoughts and feelings that would regulate your behavior. Because the beliefs contradict the rules, your behavior and decisions would be subconsciously rooted in negative connotations such as guilt, shame, unworthiness, etc, and would result in negative behavior and consequences.

All of the major religions provide the character and structure to express morals and values. How does your religion allow you to have balance? Do you have a relationship that allows you to spend time with your creator or higher power in a way that rejuvenates you, and brings about peace no matter what the circumstances?

Reconnect with your higher power. For me it's the Holy Spirit. I encourage you to embrace God as you know and understand Him. Not your mother, your father, or your grandparent's God as they know him, embrace and seek him for yourself.

It is imperative that you set aside time to spend praying, meditating, worshiping, praising, or whatever your religious practices and rituals dictate in order to connect with how you have come to know God. Begin by committing 10 – 15 minutes a day to spend in solitude. If you will commit and follow through, you will find a desire to increase that time as you grow spiritually.

How do you achieve spiritual connection? Ask yourself where did the spiritual misalignment first happen? It may be one event or circumstance, or it could be a series of events and circumstances that were within your control or not within your control.

Ask for forgiveness of any behaviors, circumstance or situation you believe caused or is causing the dissonance. You must also forgive yourself. I believe that we do the best with what we have in the moment we make a decision. In other words, in any given moment you might have to make a decision. At that time, in that moment, you will make the best possible decision you can make, be it good, bad, or indifferent. Hindsight is always 20/20, and we can always see what we could've, would've, should've done differently, but in that moment, you must remember you made the best possible decision that you could make.

Once you have asked for forgiveness, believed that you have been forgiven, and forgive yourself. Ask yourself what can you do different? If there is something you can do different write it down; and be committed to making the changes. Outline the changes step by step and ensure that they are realistic and attainable. If there is nothing you can do different, then ask yourself how can you move on? Focus on the positive aspects of moving on and write them down.

Write down how you will feel when you stop letting the memory affect your thoughts, feelings, and actions. You also have to forgive those that have harmed you intentionally or unintentionally. Why allow someone to run around rent free in your head? Forgiving does not mean that you have to allow someone that has hurt you back into your life. It means that you are releasing the pain and hurt associated with the person and their behavior. That you are choosing to move on with your life without allowing the memory or pain to dictate how you should feel, think or act.

How do you let go? We have a tendency to dwell on past hurts and disappointments. We do constant replays in our head. We talk about, cry about it, tell our friends about it over and over and over again. When you find yourself dwelling on something or someone that has hurt you, when you catch yourself living in the past, tell yourself to stop! Mid stream, right in the middle of the memory, tell yourself to stop, yell it if you have to. Sometimes it even helps to say it or yell it out loud. That will really get your attention. Tell yourself that you are not going to keep reliving the past, and mean it!

Begin to focus on what life will be like when you forgive. Write down how you will feel when you stop letting the memory affect your thoughts, feelings, and actions. Write down what your life will be like when you stop living in the past and begin to move forward. Ask for assistance from your higher power.

WRITE DOWN HOW YOU CONNECT SPIRITUALLY

HOW DO YOU KNOW YOU'RE CONNECTED?

HOW WILL YOU KNOW, OR WHEN DO YOU KNOW WHEN YOU'RE NOT CONNECTED?

USE THIS SPACE TO WRITE DOWN YOUR PLAN ON HOW YOU CAN CONTINUE TO GROW SPRITUALLY

WRITE DOWN WHAT YOUR LIFE WILL BE LIKE WHEN YOU STOP LIVING IN THE PAST AND LETTING NEGATIVE MEMORIES AFFECT YOUR THOUGHTS, FEELINGS, AND ACTION. (INCLUDE HOW YOU WILL FEEL)

IDENTIFY HOW YOU KNOW THAT YOUR LIFE HAS BEGUN TO MOVE FORWARD (IDENTIFY HOW YOU WILL FEEL)

CONTINUE TO WRITE DOWN HOW YOU WILL KNOW YOUR MOVING FORWARD

USE THIS SPACE TO WRITE ANY THOUGHTS OR AWARENESS THAT YOU HAVE HAD ABOUT YOURSELF. BEGIN THE SENTENCE WITH: I REALIZE OR NOW I UNDERSTAND...

CONTINUE TO WRITE ANY THOUGHTS OR AWARENESS YOU HAVE HAD

Chapter 6

I'm So Into You

Keep Me When I Don't Want To Be Kept

Your word says the effectual fervent prayer of the righteous availeth much, Oh Lord, keep me when I don't want to be kept.

You promised me, that through my weakness would come your strength, so when the enemy comes against me, and it seems that darkness will prevail, Oh Lord, keep me when I don't want to be kept.

As I walk the walk, and talk the talk, that I am your child, Oh Lord, keep me when I don't want to be kept.

When my spirit is willing, but my flesh is weak,
I will cry out, Not by power, Not by might, But by your Spirit, Oh Lord, keep me when I don't want to be kept.

Thy kingdom come, thy will be done,
Oh Lord, keep me when I don't want to be kept.

We are spiritual beings and are made up of three different parts: mind, body and spirit. When we look at attraction from a spiritual perspective, like spirits attract and can become entwined, creating a soul tie. Our soul is our mind, will and emotions. When a soul tie is created we become entwined with another's mind, will and emotions.

Soul ties can happen between male and female, or those of the same gender. It doesn't have to happen as a result of having sex. When two people become intimate there is a soul tie. Intimacy simply means that there is a very close association, contact or familiarity, belonging to or characterizing one's deepest nature. This can happen between friends, mentors, confidants, co-workers, family members, etc. The unity that we have with others is an expression of our soul ties. We have to open our hearts in order for a soul tie to occur.

Because we become open and vulnerable to those that we have soul ties with, if the soul tie is unhealthy it can allow for abuse, manipulation and a host of other unhealthy aspects of the relationship to occur. It can cause emotional and mental bondage that makes it difficult to honor ourselves in the relationship and our worth is compromised.

Women are emotional beings. When sex is involved it creates a more intense soul tie or union. The stronger the soul tie the deeper, the stronger the bond. The emotional and mental strengths of one sustain the other. I once heard someone say that women have sex to be loved and men love to have sex when there isn't intimacy first. If that is true, where does that leave us emotionally?

When a man and woman come together, men are the givers and women the receivers. In other words, men make a deposit and withdraw. From a biblical perspective, the bible says when man and woman come together they become one. We create a spiritual bond with each other. When you have sex with someone you not only become soul tied to that person, but to anyone else that individual has a sexual soul tie with.

Have you ever been riding down the street or just minding your own business and suddenly you have what I like to call a blast from the past? You start to reminisce or think about an old love, boyfriend or acquaintance that you haven't seen or heard from in weeks, months and sometimes even years. You have a soul tie with that individual. Although physically you have moved on, those thoughts, will and emotions are still entwined. Because there is a unique or more intense bonding that takes place when sex is involved it makes the process of leaving the relationship more difficult even when it's unhealthy.

Whether it is through sex or a close relationship with someone, we are responsible for being on guard with whom we give access to our soul. People are not always as they appear. To whom are you opening your heart, your mind, body and spirit? What checks and balances do you have in place to ensure you only allow those with well intentions toward you into your life, your space?

When you know your worth and honor your worth it prevents those that don't deserve to bond with you from entering. There will be a check in your spirit that makes you uncomfortable about that person. There will be times, or have been times, when that discomfort is subtle but still present. You may not be able to articulate or put your finger on the cause of the discomfort about that person but you will feel it all the same. That's when you know that person is not supposed to be a part of your life. Not now and sometimes not ever. That uneasiness that you feel is your spirit letting you know that person or the soul tie is not for you in that season.

You can't move forward looking back. Ask that any unhealthy soul ties be broken. If you find yourself reminiscing about an old love, or relationship, stop. It fuels the intensity of the soul tie. Focus on positive aspects of your life and begin to picture or see yourself moving forward without that person. Write down how you will move forward and what your life will look like without that person in your life. Do this with every person you have an unhealthy soul tie.

WHAT CHECKS AND BALANCES DO YOU HAVE IN PLACE OR DO YOU NEED TO PUT IN PLACE, TO ENSURE THAT YOU ONLY ALLOW THOSE WITH WELL INTENTIONS TOWARD YOU INTO YOUR LIFE? WRITE THEM DOWN

HOW ARE NEGATIVE SOUL TIES AFFECTING YOUR LIFE? WRITE THEM DOWN

WHO DO YOU NEED TO SEVER NEGATIVE UNHEALTHY SOUL TIES WITH?

WRITE DOWN WHAT YOUR LIFE WILL LOOK LIKE WITHOUT THAT SOUL TIE OR THAT PERSON IN YOUR LIFE. (HOW YOU WILL KNOW THAT YOU HAVE MOVED ON)?

CONTINUE TO WRITE DOWN HOW YOU WILL KNOW THAT YOU HAVE MOVED ON

USE THIS SPACE TO WRITE ANY THOUGHTS OR AWARENESS THAT YOU HAVE HAD ABOUT YOURSELF. BEGIN THE SENTENCE WITH: I REALIZE OR NOW I UNDERSTAND...

Chapter 7

Serenity

Stress Doesn't Live Here Any More

Stress can't live here any more. It's too much to bear. It's too much work, the stakes are too high for stress and strain to abide. Stress can't live here anymore, turmoil in my mind, my body racked with pain, strain on my soul, and for what, a bitter memory that should be no more.

Unforgiveness, guilt, and shame you no longer have a home. The hustle and bustle, no quiet time, I have no time to hear. God, I give it all to you, I'm too tired to run, stress has taken over me, stolen all my joy.

The regrets of the past, what I should have done, causes me too much stress, it's too much to bear. I give it all to you my God, those things I can't control, because stress doesn't live here any more, and I need to rest.

Thus far we have mentioned mind, body and soul, however, we have been focusing on mind and soul. What does our body have to do with balance? When we feel good on the inside we can feel good on the outside, however, usually the opposite takes place. Women often determine how they feel by how they look. A psychological study conducted in 1995 found that 3 minutes spent looking at models in a fashion magazine caused 70% of women to feel depressed, guilty and shameful. But did you know that models in magazines have been airbrushed to hide their imperfections? Society has engrained in our heads that our looks determine our worth.

The need to look a certain way, act a certain way, feel a certain way and be everything to everyone causes undo stress, as well as the demands of living life on life's terms. Becoming overwhelmed and out of balance causes undo stress. Stress is the most common cause of ill health in our society. Some studies have shown that stress is the underlying cause of 70%

of visits to the doctors' office. Some studies have also shown that constant stress has been linked to certain kinds of cancer, allergies, respiratory problems and a host of other illnesses that could be relieved or even avoided if stress was reduced.

Let's look at how the body reacts to stress. When you are stressed, your body reacts in a way that is generally termed "the fight-or-flight response". It's called fight-or-flight because internally the subconscious memories trigger a response that there is danger present. When that trigger happens, your body goes into a natural survival mode to provide the strength and energy to either fight, or run away from danger.

There is an outpouring of adrenaline into the blood stream. This, with other stress hormones, produces a number of changes in the body that are intended to be protective. The changes include an increase in heart rate and blood pressure (to get more blood to the muscles, brain and heart), faster breathing (to take in more oxygen), tensing of muscles (preparation for action), increased mental alertness and sensitivity of sense organs (to assess the situation and act quickly), increased blood flow to the brain, heart and muscles (the organs that are most important in dealing with danger) and less blood to the skin, digestive tract, kidneys and liver (where it is least needed in times of crisis).

In addition, there is an increase in blood sugar, fats and cholesterol (for extra energy) and a rise in platelets and blood clotting factors (to prevent hemorrhage in case of injury). All that is occurring in your body at any given time you allow yourself to become overwhelmed or stressed out. Your body then absorbs the increased energy because it has no outlet from the build up.

Stress can cause significant weight gain or loss, hair loss, irritability, depression, fatigue, headache, insomnia, muscle aches/stiffness (especially neck, shoulders and lower back), heart palpitations, chest pains, abdominal cramps, nausea, cold extremities, flushing or sweating and frequent colds, decrease in concentration and memory, indecisiveness, mind racing or going blank, confusion, loss of sense of humor, anxiety, nervousness, anger, frustration, worry, fear, irritability, impatience, short temper, smoking, drinking, crying, yelling, swearing, blaming, throwing things or hitting and a host of other internal and external negative consequences to the body.

We experience what I call "good stress" and "bad stress". An example of "good stress" would be when you're planning for a joyous occasion or event. "Bad stress" would be when there is a problem or situation that has taken a front seat in your life and you would rather it not be there. Be it good or bad, your body still reacts in the same manner (the fight-or flight-response). I'll say it again, when you're physically out of balance you are mentally and spiritually out of balance.

Stress is inevitable. The key is learning to manage your stress by creating outlets for the energy created in the fight-or flight-stage. An outlet is created by temporarily taking your mind off of whatever is causing stress. You can always revisit the issue when you feel revived, rested and in a better frame of mind. Here are a few ways of managing stress:

- ❖ Well-balanced diet.
- ❖ Regular exercise, (at least 30 minutes, three times per week).
- ❖ Adequate sleep, (figure out what you need, then get it).
- ❖ Look at things more positively.
- ❖ See problems as opportunities.
- ❖ Refute negative thoughts.
- ❖ Keep a sense of humor (Take time to laugh).
- ❖ Leisure time (do something for yourself everyday even if it's only 15 minutes).
- ❖ Relaxation exercises (meditation, listening to music).
- ❖ Time and money management.
- ❖ Assertiveness.
- ❖ Problem-solving.
- ❖ Possibly leaving a job or a relationship.

Take time out (anything from a short walk to a vacation) to get away from the things that are bothering you. This will not resolve the problem, but it gives you a break and a chance for your stress levels to decrease.

When you take care of your stress, you take care of your body. When your body is in tune and balanced you have the ability to think clearly and make better decisions. It also allows you the ability to focus on your spiritual nourishment because you are more open to hear and receive spiritual guidance.

How do you begin to manage stress? You first have to identify your stressors. Begin with the list above on how your body reacts to stress. You may even be able to identify some that are not on the list. Write them down.

Develop a plan to manage your stress in each area that you determine is a stressor for you. You can begin with the list above or make your own. Think about what is fun for you, something that you could easily incorporate into your lifestyle that would only take 15- 20 minutes a day and write it down. Begin to imagine or focus on your life free of stress or with minimal stress. Write down what would that look like for you?

If you're not already practicing stress management, you want to start with small, realistic, attainable, baby steps (you don't want to increase your stress by trying to follow a plan to manage your stress and become even more overwhelmed). If you already have some stress management techniques in place, consider how you can continue to build and strengthen what is already working for you.

In chapter five I talked about forgiving as an important aspect of your spirituality. Studies have been able to show links between unforgiveness with various physical illnesses and certain cancers. When you refuse to forgive those that have wronged you, you hold on to the pain and the emotions of that hurt. Much like stress works in the body, so does unforgiveness.

When you refuse to forgive it creates anger, guilt, stress and other intense emotions or energy for which there is no outlet. You're like a pressure cooker ready to blow, however you never release all the steam. Your mind, body and spirit are in a constant state of conflict.

I once worked with a client who had been the victim of overwhelming amounts of racism. Although his anger was understandable and justifiable, he refused to forgive those that had wronged him. He was always angry and had constant triggers to remind him of how unfairly he had been treated. By the time he came to see me his subconscious memories were constantly being triggered, and he was unable to distinguish between real and imagined acts of racism toward him. Because he was holding on to the trauma of the events that had happened to him and refused to forgive, he was constantly reliving the experience.

He was in his early 40's, had major heart trouble, his hair was falling out and he was experiencing panic attacks. Imagine to his surprise the peace that he felt when he started to forgive. What he realized was that forgiving wasn't excusing those that had treated him poorly, nor did it justify what they had done. Most important he realized that forgiving didn't minimize his experience. His health improved and he stopped having panic attacks.

The most important way to manage stress and to forgive is to remember to surrender those things you have no control over and to let go of the things you can't change.

USE THIS SPACE TO WRITE YOUR STRESS MANAGEMENT PLAN

USE THIS SPACE TO WRITE YOUR THOUGHTS ABOUT FORGIVING

WHO DO YOU NEED TO FORGIVE? BEGIN THE SENTENCE WITH: I FORGIVE...

HOW WILL YOU KNOW YOU HAVE FORGIVEN THEM? WRITE IT DOWN

WRITE DOWN WHAT LIFE WILL BE LIKE WHEN YOU FORGIVE

Chapter 8

Moving Out of Your Comfort Zone

A Familiar Place

It seems that I've been down this road before, twist and turns seem forever more. In the mirror I see a familiar face, yet somehow, I don't know you at all. A distant voice, a familiar sound, yet somehow, you're a stranger to me.

The eyes they seem to keep speaking to me, something of familiarity. Although I know you, I don't know you at all. Yep, it seems that I've been down this road before.

What is your comfort zone? Webster defines comfort zone as the level at which one functions with ease and familiarity. Familiarity is defined as close acquaintance with something or someone. Your comfort zone is that place where you dwell that is familiar to you. Be it good bad or indifferent, you continue to function, think and act from that place of familiarity because it's comfortable for you.

Your thoughts, behavior and actions become routine. You respond to situations, thoughts, behavior and attitude without thinking about what's taking place because it has become routine or habit. What happens when you are accustomed to chaos, confusion, hurt, guilt, anger, pain, frustration, etc., and you add familiarity? You become acquainted with dysfunction. As a result of dysfunction, you continue to have chaos, confusion, hurt, guilt, anger, pain, frustration, etc., which then becomes your comfort zone.

Let me give you an example of how this all comes together. I worked with a client that continued to find herself with what she termed as "the wrong men". In her relationships she never came first and was always taken for granted. She disclosed that although she would be disrespected, used and sometimes abused, it was always the man that would end the relationship.

She struggled with letting go, or ending the relationship even when she saw the relationship taking a turn for the worst. Even when she could see that the person she was dating did not respect or appreciate her, she continued to hold on. Intellectually she knew she deserved better but she always seemed to choose men that didn't value or honor her worth.

She requested counseling because she couldn't understand why or how she continued to find herself in similar circumstances. After looking at her track record and her history, she discovered that she had never dealt with an issue of abandonment.

When she was a little girl she and her father were close. She was daddy's little girl. Then one day he suddenly left her mother and her for another woman. As a result of his leaving, he wouldn't have anything to do with her. What she discovered was because of that experience she subconsciously made several decisions.

The first decision was that he didn't love her or he wouldn't have left. The second decision was that no one would ever leave her again unless it was on her terms. The third decision was that if the man loved her, he would stay no matter what, even if it meant she had to put up with him seeing other women. As long as he came back to her she was willing to compromise. The man would eventually end the relationship, which continued creating a vicious cycle of pain and feelings of abandonment.

She discovered that because she had never had closure, the pain of the abandonment was her comfort zone. She would choose men of a particular character, or create situations in which the men in her life would eventually leave. Although no one likes pain, if pain is the place where you dwell, you will continue to create situations or circumstances for pain because it is what you have grown accustomed to. It is what you know.

Your comfort zone doesn't have to begin from a place of pain but as a result can end up in a place of pain. That pain can then become your comfort zone. Your comfort zone can be any behavior, attitude, or a certain way of thinking that you have made decisions about, sometimes consciously, but most often subconsciously. Often times because that behavior, attitude or way of thinking has become routine, you function from that place of subconscious thinking. Even when others can see that the decisions you make are self-defeating, you continue to operate from that place because it is what you know and what you are comfortable with.

Take an alcoholic for example: There are many different ways an alcoholic makes the decision or comes to the belief that alcohol works for them. I have heard many reasons as to why someone drinks excessively and what it does for him or her. From helping to relieve stress, to helping them forget…(you fill in the blank), to it helps them cope. That learning can take place growing up in an alcoholic environment, or it can be as simple as taking your first drink and discovering that it can change an undesired mood or state of mind, to a desired mood or state of mind.

Once the decision is made (consciously or subconsciously) that alcohol can assist in achieving the desired state, it becomes habit to use it for the purpose or purposes the person drinking is trying to achieve. That habit then becomes an addiction.

But let's look at it before it becomes an addiction. What the person learns is that this is the way to achieve the desired mood or state of mind that they want to have. Even though the drinking may begin to cause problems long before it becomes an addiction, the person drinking can't see that alcohol is the problem. They have already decided that the alcohol helps them to achieve the desired mood or state of mind. So they continue to drink. In turn, the drinking continues to create more problems, and so they drink to deal with the problems. It becomes a vicious cycle … their comfort zone.

How often do you think about what you're thinking about? That was a mouth full. When you think about what you are thinking about, you pause and search to find out what you're basing a decision on. When the client that I described above stopped to think about what she was thinking about, (in other words, when she stopped to look at why she continued to choose the same type of men), she discovered it was from a place of hurt and distorted views about how to choose a mate. Even more important was her decision on how she believed that person showed her that he loved her. Because the decision and the belief about love were distorted, her decisions were distorted and she created a vicious cycle of pain and abandonment.

It is imperative to remember that you are not responsible for someone else's actions. When you choose to let others define your worth you create a foundation of fear and make unhealthy or distorted decisions from that fear. How are you allowing someone else's actions to define your worth?

When you operate from a comfort zone of fear it prohibits you from making clear decisions, and distorts your thoughts, beliefs and behaviors.

How does your comfort zone sabotage your progress? How do you begin to identify what you are thinking about that has become familiar and comfortable to you?

Begin by identifying those fears…fear of abandonment, guilt shame, stress, etc. Then ask yourself when was the first time you ever experienced that feeling? When was the first time you felt abandoned, hurt, and guilty, etc.? Identify the feeling or feelings associated with the fear; pain, disappointment, anger, etc. Write them down.

In chapter two we discussed when you operate from a place of fear it dictates your behavior, beliefs and attitude. You also learned that fear is associated with your feelings. Ask yourself what you need to do to resolve those feelings associated with fear? Do you need to forgive? Is it something that you had control over? Can you change what happened? When you think about the situation or feelings, replace the feelings of hurt, pain, etc with feelings of love, respect, honor, and worth.

Begin to think outside the box. What do I mean by that? Begin to imagine and see yourself in the same situation but with a different outcome. Focus on how you would like the next set of circumstances or situation to have a different outcome.

For example, my client made a list of her attributes and worth and made the decision that she wouldn't compromise. She made another list of what she wanted from her mate. What qualities and attributes he had to have, how he would treat her, what she was willing to compromise (nobody is perfect), and what she wouldn't compromise. When she met someone, she would compare her lists to what the person revealed about himself. If he didn't meet those qualities and attributes on her list, and if it wasn't a quality or attribute she was willing to compromise, she would move on.

WHAT IS YOUR COMFORT ZONE?

DO YOU CONTINUE TO FIND YOURSELF IN SIMILAR SITUATIONS THAT YOU WOULD LIKE TO CHANGE? IF SO WHAT ARE THEY?

IF YOU CONTINUE TO DO WHAT YOU HAVE ALWAYS DONE. YOU'LL CONTINUE TO GET WHAT YOU HAVE ALWAYS GOTTEN. WHAT DO YOU NEED TO DIFFERENT TO GET DIFFERENT RESULTS. BEGIN YOUR SENTENCE WITH: I WILL DO (FILL IN THE BLANK) DIFFERENT BY.....

CONTINUE TO WRITE WHAT YOU'LL DO DIFFERENT

USE THIS SPACE TO WRITE ANY THOUGHTS OR AWARENESS THAT YOU HAVE HAD ABOUT YOURSELF. BEGIN THE SENTENCE WITH: I REALIZE OR NOW I UNDERSTAND…

Chapter 9

Bringing It All Together

A Woman of Worth

Who says that I can't have it all, when I'm all that I can be? A woman with skill, style and grace, I'm a virtuous woman, a woman of worth, with ease so naturally.

Who says that I can't be it all, all that I'm call to be? I'm resourceful, an achiever there's no other way, I'm a woman of worth, with out any doubts that I'm all that I am to be.

I walk with confidence and such finesse; you say how do I manage it all? I do it with ease and amazing grace; I'm every woman I need to be. It didn't happen by happenstance, I choose my words carefully. I mean what I say and say what I mean, I think before I speak. No time for second-guessing myself, I'm a woman of worth, so don't you see, I do it naturally.

Who says that I can't do it all, be the virtuous woman I'm suppose to be? A virtuous woman, a woman of worth, my value is beyond compare. I'm brilliant and gorgeous within my own right, my secrets I can not share, but isn't it obvious who I am, I'm who God created me to be. I'm a woman of worth and it comes so naturally.

How do you begin to bring it all together? Webster defines virtuous as potent, efficacious (having the power to produce a desired affect), having or exhibiting virtue, moral excellence, righteous, chaste or chastity in a woman, valor, a beneficial quality or power of a thing. How do you become a virtuous woman, a woman of worth? The poem describes the ideal woman as one whose life is centered on God (mind, body and spirit). By focusing on and incorporating all that you have learned, you will begin the journey of becoming a woman of worth.

I remember spending one summer with my grandmother. Every morning I would wake up to her blasting this old gospel song. The verse said: Lord, don't move my mountain, but give me the strength to climb, and Lord, you don't have to take away my stumbling block, but lead me all around it.

As I think back on that song, I realize that the singer was saying that as she lived life on life's terms there are going to be experiences in life that we can't avoid, that we have no control over. Lessons that we need to learn in order to serve out our purpose. However, those lessons aren't going to always be comfortable, or pleasant. But, instead of focusing on the how uncomfortable the experience is, let me see it as a lesson that's here to teach me something, that is here to help me move to the next level, or to help me take the next step in this journey we call life. Instead of dwelling on the negative, let me learn the lesson that has presented itself in my life. Instead of continuing to go around the bottom of the mountain, give me the strength to climb, to take one more step toward my goal (my purpose). The stumbling blocks are the obstacles of life, teach me how to overcome them.

As you begin to move toward who you are called to be, remember, whatever you think, whatever you say, so be it. If you use words like can't, won't never in a negative way, so be it. If you say you can't, you won't, if you say you'll never be successful, you won't. But, if you focus on your purpose, you'll walk in your purpose because you'll attract who you are and what you believe. So, what do you believe? How do you begin to walk in your purpose? You already know.

- Recognize or identify your strengths? What are they? What do you like to do? What is your passion?
- Admit your shortcomings. It's ok if you're not good at everything, focus on the things that you are good at.
- Stop beating yourself up about all the woulda, coulda, shoulda's in your life. When I catch myself thinking those thoughts, I always pray, let me learn this lesson

now so that I don't have to go around this mountain again, teach me how to climb it.
- Appreciate, accept, and respect the needs of the people around you.
- Try new ideas and behaviors.
- Risk failing? There I said it, I said the F word! It's ok to fail! Sometimes experience is the best teacher. Learn from your experiences and move forward using the new knowledge you've gained?
- Treat yourself and others with kindness and compassion.

To be honest with others you have to be honest with yourself. How have you subconsciously made decisions that have had negative consequences for yourself and others? Although sometimes painful to confront and even harder to do something about, there is no time better than the present. Or you can choose to continue to operate from a place of unhealthy decisions.

Who's the center of your life? Where do you get your spiritual nourishment? How do you connect with God as you know him? What practices do you have in place to have a constant, ongoing connection? Seek him, as you know him. Ask for guidance.

Any time there is change, certain questions should be answered. Who, what, when, how, and why? Who will the changes affect? What will be the benefit or the consequences? How will the changes take place? When will they take place (will it be immediate or will there be a process). How will they take place? Why does the change need to happen?

Remember to **think about what you're thinking about.** Be careful what you speak, words like always, never, and should, etc used in a negative way will bring about negative results. How have negative thoughts, feelings and behaviors prevented you from letting your own light shine? What are the opposites of those negative thoughts, feelings and behaviors? Write them down.

Who has hurt you and how can you bring about peace and reconciliation for yourself? Remember to accept the things you cannot change, or have no control over, commit to changing the things that you can change, and pray for the wisdom to know the difference.

What perception or belief do you have about yourself? What are your values and are they in alignment with your beliefs and behaviors? What parts of you are still operating from a place of brokenness?

What unhealthy relationships or soul ties do you need to sever? How have they prevented you from moving forward? How can you begin to move forward?

Write down where you are (Self-defeating beliefs and behaviors). Where do you want to go? (Positive thoughts and behaviors). If you woke up tomorrow and could have your life just the way you wanted it, what would it look like? Write it down and really focus on the positive aspects of your life.

Who do you want to be as a mother, daughter, sister, friend, co-worker, boss, confidant, teacher, etc.? Write down each role you have or want to have. What would those roles look like? Who would they affect? Where does your spirituality and religion fit into those roles? Write down what changes you want to make in your thinking and behavior and the necessary steps to make those changes.

How do you get there? Write down detailed, realistic, attainable goals for each area of your life and then develop a plan to begin making the changes you want to make. In no time you can become that virtuous woman, because you will know that your worth is far beyond the price of rubies, the woman you're called to be.

YOUR TIME IS NOW. DO YOU KNOW YOUR PURPOSE? WHAT IS IT?

**ARE YOU WALKING IN THAT PURPOSE?
IF YES, HOW DO YOU KNOW? IF NOT, WHY NOT?**

USE THIS SPACE TO WRITE ANY THOUGHTS OR AWARENESS THAT YOU HAVE HAD ABOUT YOURSELF. BEGIN THE SENTENCE WITH: I REALIZE OR NOW I UNDERSTAND...

The exercises on the following pages can be done individually or in small groups.

THE ROSE

THE ROSE UNIVERSALLY SYMBOLIZES LOVE AND BEAUTY. IN ORDER FOR A ROSE TO GROW IT MUST TO BE PLACED IN AN ENVIRONMENT THAT WILL CULTIVATE ITS GROWTH. IT REQUIRES PRUNING TO RID ITSELF OF PARTS THAT NO LONGER SERVE ITS PURPOSE. IT REQUIRES LIGHT AS A SOURCE OF ENERGY TO BRING FORTH ITS BEAUTY TO SHOW TO THE WORLD.

IN ORDER FOR YOU TO COME FORTH AS A SYMBOL OF LOVE AND BEAUTY, YOU MUST PLANT YOURSELF IN ENVIRONMENTS THAT WILL CULTIVATE YOUR GROWTH. YOU MUST REFLECT ON THE PARTS THAT BLOCK YOUR LIGHT, AND PRUNE THOSE PARTS THAT NO LONGER SERVE YOU. IT IS THEN, THROUGH YOUR SOURCE OF ENERGY, YOUR LIGHT, THAT YOU WILL REFLECT YOUR PURPOSE AND BRING FORTH YOUR BEAUTY TO SHOW THE WORLD.

DESCRIBE WHAT YOU WILL DO TO BECOME LIKE THE ROSE

HOW WILL YOU PLANT YOURSELF IN ENVIRONMENTS THAT WILL CONTINUE TO CULTIVATE YOUR GROWTH?

WHAT ARE THE AREAS IN YOUR LIFE THAT BLOCK YOUR LIGHT?

HOW WILL YOU PRUNE THOSE PARTS THAT NO LONGER SERVE YOU?

CONTINUE TO WRITE HOW YOU WILL PRUNE THOSE PARTS THAT NO LONGER SERVE YOU

USE THIS SPACE TO WRITE DOWN WHAT YOUR LIFE WOULD LOOK LIKE IF YOU COULD HAVE IT JUST THE WAY YOU WANT IT (BE SPECIFIC)

CONTINUE WRITING WHAT YOU WANT YOUR LIFE TO BE

USE THIS SPACE TO WRITE DOWN WHAT CHANGES YOU WANT TO MAKE IN YOUR THINKING. BEGIN THE SENTENCE WITH: THE CHANGES I WILL MAKE IN MY THINKING ARE ...

CONTINUE TO WRITE DOWN WHAT CHANGES YOU WILL MAKE IN THE WAY YOU THINK

USE THIS SPACE TO WRITE DOWN WHAT CHANGES YOU WANT TO MAKE IN YOUR BEHAVIOR. BEGIN THE SENTENCE WITH: THE CHANGES I WILL MAKE IN MY BEHAVIOR ARE…

CONTINUE TO WRITE WHAT CHANGES YOU'LL MAKE IN YOUR BEHAVIOR

THERE IS AN OLD SAYING, THE MORE THINGS CHANGE THE MORE THEY STAY THE SAME.

CHANGE IS INEVITABLE, THE QUESTION TO ASK YOURSELF: HAS THERE BEEN GROWTH AS THINGS HAVE CHANGED, OR HAVE THEY REMAINED THE SAME?

ON THE FOLLOWING PAGES ANSWER THE QUESTIONS ABOUT GROWTH.

AS CHANGE HAS HAPPENED IN YOUR LIFE, WHAT THINGS HAVE REMAINED THE SAME?

AS GROWTH HAPPENS, WHAT WILL BE DIFFERENT IN YOUR LIFE?

AS YOU GROW, WHO WILL THE CHANGES AFFECT?

WHAT WILL BE THE BENEFITS OR THE CONSEQUENCES OF THAT GROWTH FOR YOU?

WHAT WILL BE THE BENEFITS OR THE CONSEQUENCES OF THAT GROWTH FOR OTHERS IN YOUR LIFE?

HOW WILL YOU NURTURE YOUR GROWTH?

CONTINUE TO WRITE HOW YOU WILL NUTURE YOUR GROWTH

WHAT GROWTH WILL YOU SEE IMMEDIATELY?

WHAT GROWTH WILL HAPPEN OVER TIME?

USE THIS SPACE TO WRITE DOWN NECESSARY STEPS TO FOR CHANGE IN ORDER TO BEGIN TO GROW

HOW WILL YOU KNOW WHEN GROWTH IS HAPPENING?

USE THIS SPACE TO WRITE DOWN WHAT YOUR LIFE WILL BE LIKE ONCE YOU MAKE THE CHANGES YOU JUST WROTE ABOUT. BEGIN THE SENTENCE WITH: THE GROWTH THAT I MAKE WILL ALLOW MY LIFE TO BE...

CONTINUE TO WRITE WHAT YOUR LIFE WILL BE LIKE ONCE YOU BEGIN TO GROW

HOW WILL YOU CONTINUE TO MONITOR YOUR PLAN FOR GROWTH TO ENSURE GROWTH IS CONTINUING TO HAPPEN?

www.ingramcontent.com/pod-product-compliance
Lightning Source LLC
LaVergne TN
LVHW051605070426
835507LV00021B/2787